W9-DIN-750

THOSE PRECIOUS PRANKSTERS,
EGGBERT AND EGGBERTA,
SPEAK OUT FROM THE INSIDE!

Here's an all-new collection of wit and wisdom from those two irrepressible cartoon characters who have not yet entered this earthly paradise. From their unique vantage point, they observe the ways of the world that will soon be theirs—especially the ways of expectant parents.

Books by LAF

Eggbert: Belly Laughs
Eggbert Easy Over
Eggbert: Funny Side Up
Scrambled Eggbert
Strictly Fresh Eggbert

Published by POCKET BOOKS

 *Are there paperbound books you want
but cannot find in your retail stores?*

You can get any title in print in **POCKET BOOK** editions. Simply
send retail price, local sales tax, if any, plus 35¢ per book to
cover mailing and handling costs, to:

MAIL SERVICE DEPARTMENT
POCKET BOOKS • A Division of Simon & Schuster, Inc.
1 West 39th Street • New York, New York 10018

Please send check or money order. We cannot be responsible
for cash.   *Catalogue sent free on request.*

Titles in this series are also available at discounts in quantity
lots for industrial or sales-promotional use. For details write our
Special Projects Agency: The Benjamin Company, Inc., 485
Madison Avenue, New York, New York 10022.

Eggbert
Easy Over

Cartoons by LAF

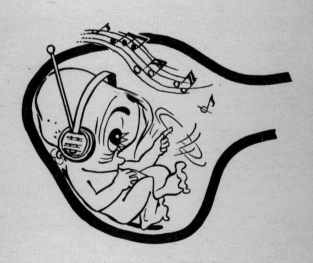

PUBLISHED BY POCKET BOOKS NEW YORK

EGGBERT EASY OVER

POCKET BOOK edition published October, 1976

This original POCKET BOOK edition is printed from brand-new plates made from newly set, clear, easy-to-read type. POCKET BOOK editions are published by POCKET BOOKS, a division of Simon & Schuster, Inc., A GULF+WESTERN COMPANY 630 Fifth Avenue, New York, N.Y. 10020. Trademarks registered in the United States and other countries.

2 3 7 6

ISBN: 0-671-80753-6.

Copyright, ©, 1976, by LAF. All rights reserved.

Printed in the U.S.A.

Eggbert
Easy Over

"EVER GET THE FEELING
LIFE'S PASSING YOU BY?"

"WAKE UP, MOM! I HEAR HIM SNEAKIN' UP THE BACK STAIRS!"

" SHHHHH!
MOM'S PLAYIN' A VULNERABLE
GRAND SLAM DOUBLED!"

"NO WAY!
SHE COULDN'T BE PREGNANT!
OR <u>COULD</u> SHE?"

" I GOTTA SMARTEN UP FAST!
THEY SOUND KINDA
RUTHLESS OUT THERE!"

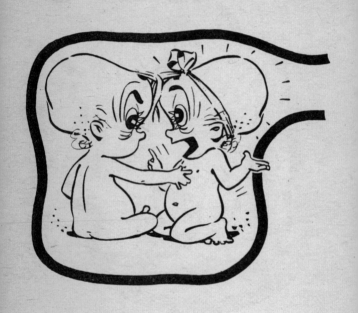

"MAYBE IF I PUSH THIS BUTTON,
IT'LL TURN HER OFF!"

"SURE WISH POP WOULD
BUY MOM A BLENDER!"

" DAMN IT, MOM...
FASTEN OUR SEAT BELT!"

"ORDER THE FULL COURSE, MOM —
THE CHEAPSKATE HASN'T DINED
US OUT IN A <u>MONTH</u>! "

"YIPPEE-DO-DAH!
SHE'S GONNA KEEP US!"

"LOVE? FORGET IT!
MARRY FOR MONEY!"

" WE SURE PICKED A HORSE
WITH A SWEET GAIT!"

"YOU THINK I'M COMIN' OUT
TO CLEAN UP YOUR MESS?
NO WAY!"

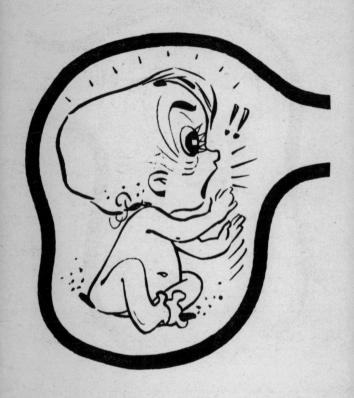

"...AN' ALSO REMIND HIM THIS IS
NO TIME TO BAD-MOUTH HIS BOSS!"

" IF I KNEW WHERE I CAME FROM,
I'D GO BACK ! "

"IF WE PLAY IT COOL WHEN
WE GET OUT, THEY'LL WAIT ON US
HAND AND FOOT!"

"...BECAUSE IF THIS WERE AN EGG,
YOU'D HEAR MOM CACKLE!"

" WONDER WHY POP LETS OUT
SUCH A SAD SIGH
WHEN MOM GETS INTO BED ? "

" WHAT DO YA MEAN... 'YOU WONDER
WHAT'S IN THE NEXT ROOM' "?

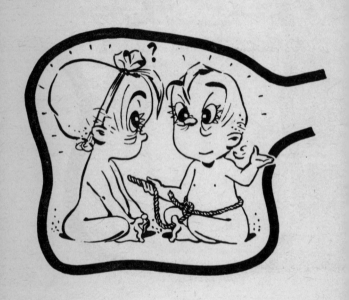

"TWO JERKS MEANS IT'S SAFE
TO COME OUT!"

"WHEN DID I GET HERE...
JULY OR AUGUST?"

" IF IT'S GONNA COST A THOUSAND
BUCKS TO GET US OUT OF HERE...
WE'RE AN ENDANGERED SPECIES ! "

" YOU'D THINK AT LEAST ONE OF THESE
COLD MORNINGS <u>HE'D</u> GET UP
AND GET THE <u>PAPER</u> ! "

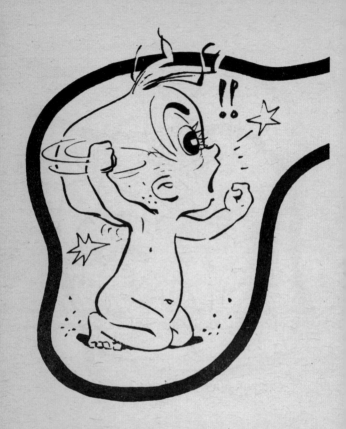

" TRY THAT ONCE MORE, DOC, AND
THEY'LL BE CALLING YOU
FOUR-FINGER-FREDDIE ! "

"COME ON! MY TIME TO SIT ON THE SHADY SIDE!"

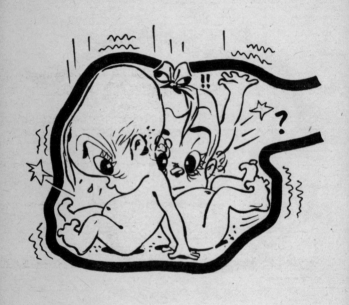

" MAN, WHEN HER BACK POOPS OUT,
. . . DISASTERVILLE, U.S.A. ! "

"GESUNDHEIT, MOM... AND KEEP AWAY FROM THAT DAMN GOLDENROD!"

" 'BLESSED GIFT FROM HEAVEN', FATHER RYAN CALLS ME. HE'D CHANGE HIS TUNE IF HE CAUGHT HER ON A BILIOUS MORNING!"

"ONE OF HER QUEASY DAYS, FOLKS!"

" WISH SHE'D LAY OFF THOSE
CRUNCHY CEREALS! "

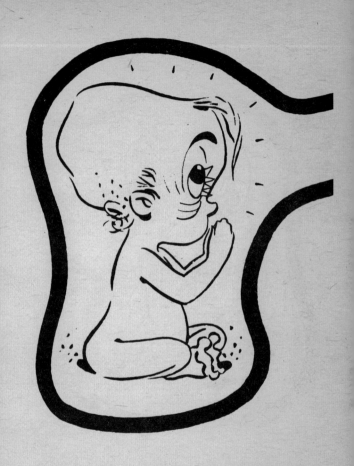

"...AND PLEASE PUT A LITTLE LOVE
INTO PEOPLE BEFORE YOU
WHISTLE ME OUT!"

" RIGHT ON, MOMSY-POO. LESH HAVE
ONE FOR THA ROAD! "

" SUPPOSE I CAME OUT AND
NOBODY WAS THERE ? "

" NO WAY! YOU JUST DON'T
POP OUT AND YELL 'SURPRISE'!"

" YEH, MAYBE SCIENCE HAS US ALL
FIGURED OUT...BUT <u>ASK</u> 'EM
WHO STARTS OUR MOTOR ! "

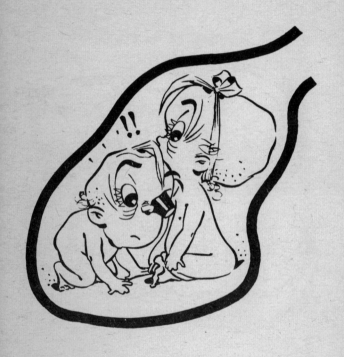

" SORRY, KID...IT'S JUST A PIMPLE! "

"YOUR RED HAIR COMES FROM A RECESSIVE
GENE THAT... AW, FORGET IT... YOU
PROBABLY LOOK LIKE YOUR MOTHER!"

"SOON AS SHE GETS THE BREAKFAST TRAY ON HER LAP... BOMBS AWAY!"

" WONDER WHAT KIND
OF A SNACK WE'RE GONNA SEND
HIM OUT FOR TONIGHT?"

"MAMA MIA,
THOSE ITALIANS PINCH DEEP!"

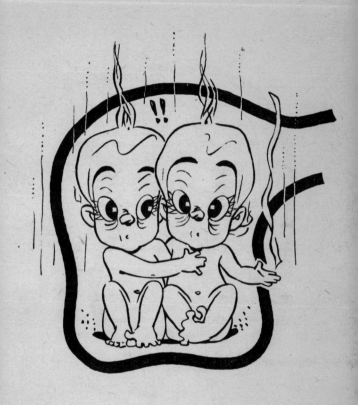

" THEIR NEW WATERBED'S GREAT...
UNTIL POP GETS RESTLESS! "

"IT'S RIGHT PLEASING TO WATCH
A LITTLE SEX MACHINE DEVELOP!"

" SO SHE'S MAD AT <u>HIM</u>.
WHY TAKE IT OUT ON <u>ME</u> ?"

" I THINK THE ENERGY CRUNCH
FINALLY HIT MOM! "

" FAR OUT, MOM! ORDER IT!
WE HAVEN'T HAD A HOT FUDGE SUNDAE
IN MONTHS! "

" I JUST CAN'T GET OVER THE FEELING
I'VE BEEN THROUGH THIS BEFORE! "

" GOIN' SOMEWHERE? "

"JUST IN CASE YOU CHANGE YOUR MIND...
HOW YOU GONNA GET BACK?"

"ONE MORE MINUTE IN THIS STEAMROOM AND SHE CAN SERVE ME POACHED WITH HOLLANDAISE!"

" JUST JET-LAG, FOLKS... "

"GUESS WHO!"

" WHEN THERE'S HAPPINESS UPSTAIRS...
THERE'S HAPPINESS DOWNSTAIRS! "

" BATTEN DOWN THE HATCHES!
SHE'S BUILDIN' UP TO A GOOD CRY!"

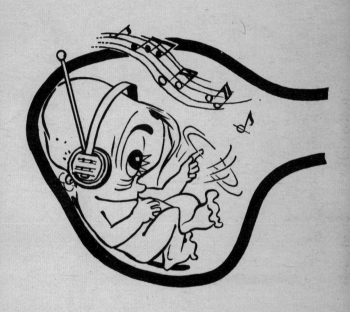

"MUSTA' BEEN GRIM FOR KIDS
GOIN' THROUGH THIS WITHOUT
TODAY'S CONVENIENCES!"

"I DON'T MIND THE GURGLES. IT'S THE CHUGGING THAT GETS ME DOWN!"

"AFTER ALL THE GOODIES MOM SENDS DOWN HERE...BABY FOOD...YUK!"

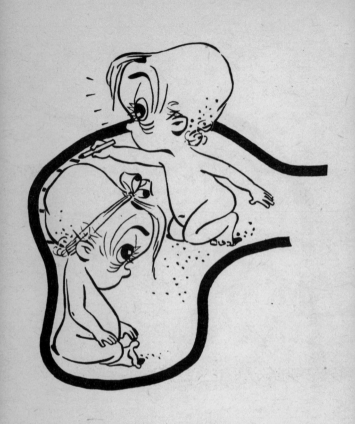

"LOOKS LIKE YOU
GREW ANOTHER QUARTER INCH!"

" WHEN HE RAIDS THE FRIDGE
BARE FOOTED... WHY WARM UP ON US? "

"WOW! THE TALK THAT GOES ON
IN A GYNECOLOGIST'S WAITING ROOM!"

"ENJOY EVERY MINUTE DOWN HERE...
SOUNDS LIKE THINGS ARE
ROUGHER THAN A COB OUT THERE!"

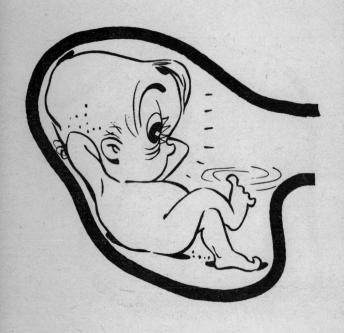

" LIFE'S BEEN PRETTY GOOD TO ME,
SO FAR !"

" WHOEVER NAMED MOM 'LAZY SUSAN'
WAS RIGHT ON! "

" THOSE DAMN SOAP OPERAS SHE LISTENS
TO ALL DAY ARE BUGGIN' ME! "

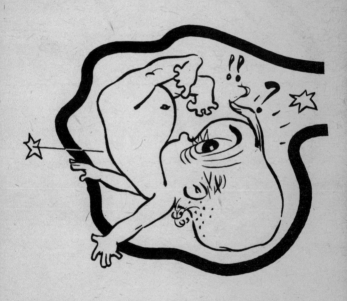

"SEEMS TO ME SHE ISN'T BOWLIN'
TONIGHT WITH HER USUAL FINESSE!"

" THIS IS A HELL OF A TIME
FOR HER TO TAKE UP BELLY-DANCIN' ! "

" WHAT A BLAST IF I COULD COME OUT
WEARIN' A BEARD ! "

" PLAN ALL YOU WANT! I'M GOING TO LIVE MY OWN LIFE – AN' THAT'S _THAT_! "

"KINDA CHOPPY ON THE BAY TODAY,
I IMAGINE!"

" THIS PAD LOOKS BRAND NEW TO ME.
GUESS I'M NUMBER 1. "

" ...SO, SNOW WHITE TOOK ONE BITE OF
THE APPLE AN'...AN' I'M GETTIN' DAMN
SICK OF REPEATING THIS STUPID YARN!"

"MUST BE SAVING ME FOR
SOMETHIN' IMPORTANT OUT THERE!"

" DON'T TELL _ME_ YOU GOTTA GO...
CALL YOUR MOTHER ! "

" YELL UP AND ASK MOM
WHEN DINNER'S READY ! "

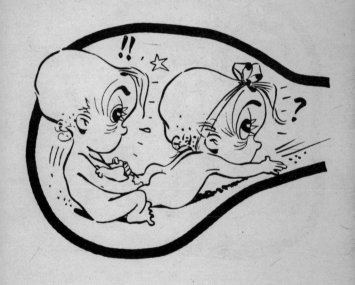

"...AND THAT AIN'T ALL L'IL KANGAROOS CAN DO THAT <u>YOU</u> CAN'T!"

"POP'S A HORNY OLD GOAT,
<u>ISN'T</u> HE?"

"WOW! CAN SHE WHIP UP
THE NIGHTMARES!"

" BOY, SHE SURE LIKES HER
WHISKEY SOURS . . . _SOUR!_ "

" TAKE YOUR TIME, DOC. WE THINK
IT'S PEACHY TO SIT AROUND NAKED
WHILE YOU HAVE YOUR COFFEE BREAK! "

"ANOTHER GAWDAM CRIB TOY
THAT PLAYS BRAHMS' LULLABY!"

" SURE I'M THE SPITTIN' IMAGE OF GRANPA... <u>NO TEETH</u>! "

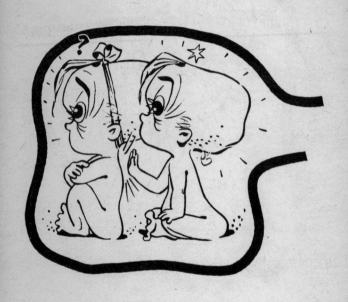

" DON'T SWEAT IT. WHOEVER PUT US IN
KNOWS HOW TO GET US OUT! "

" WHATCHA EXPECT FROM A
RED-BLOODED KID? GO PUT SOME
CLOTHES ON OR SOMETHIN' ! "

" NEGATIVE. JUST GAS!"

"LEAVE IT TO POP. HE CAN'T GET
THE BUCKLE AROUND MOM...
AND THE DAMN CAR WON'T START!"

" WISH WE COULD SEE POP IN THE
MEN'S ROOM WHEN HE FINDS
HE PUT ON MOM'S PANTS! "

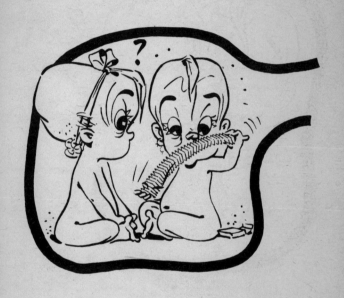

" SURE, PLENTY OF TIME FOR A FAST
GAME OR TWO OF GIN *!* "

" DAMNED IF SHE DIDN'T CRAWL OUT
WITH A WINNING HAND OF GIN ! "

"AWRIGHT ALREADY! WE GOT 2 HOURS
BEFORE THEY CHARGE OVERTIME!"

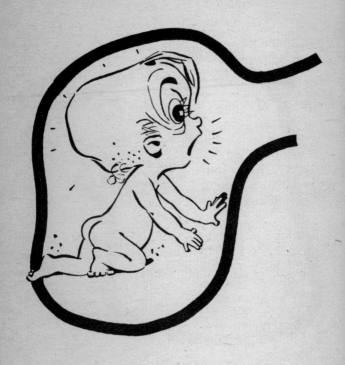

" RELAX, MOM . . . I'M TAKING IT
ALONE FROM HERE ! "